Learning Language Through Movement

Learning Language Through Movement

Practical games, exercises and activities

Garry Powell and Debra Armstrong

Copyright © Garry Powell and Debra Armstrong 2022

All rights reserved. No part of this book may be reproduced or transmitted in any form or by any means, electronic or mechanical, including photocopying, recording or by any information storage and retrieval system, without prior permission in writing from the publisher.

Published by Amba Press
Melbourne, Australia
www.ambapress.com.au

Cover designer – Tess McCabe

Printed by IngramSpark

ISBN: 9781922607300 (pbk)
ISBN: 9781922607317 (ebk)

A catalogue record for this book is available from the National Library of Australia.

About the authors

Garry Powell was a teacher and administrator in both city and regional Australian government schools throughout his career. He spent much of his time as a classroom teacher, specialist physical education teacher and principal at inner city schools. He lectured in tertiary education for years, and has spoken on teacher education at conferences and workshops. Garry now spends his time writing teacher education resources and physical education content for children. He is the author of numerous books and resources.

Debra Armstrong taught in government primary and specialist schools for most of her career. She was a classroom teacher and an art and physical education specialist teacher. She has won various awards, fellowships and lectured at Monash University. Debra is an experienced co-author who has written a number of teacher resources.

Contents

Introduction	1
Section one: single-word concepts	**3**
start/stop	4
up/down	6
above/below	8
right/left	10
top/bottom	12
forward/backward	14
inside/outside	16
before/after	18
same/different	20
to/from	22
front/behind	24
on/under	26
over/next to	28
thin/wide	30
big/small	32
high/low	34
hard/soft	36
slow/fast	38
begin/end	40
once/again	42
first/last	44
second/third	46
whole/part	48
all/half	50
more/less	52
almost/as many	54
corner/row	56
with/at	58
across/diagonal	60
straight/curved	62
match/mirror	64
through/between	66
side/middle	68
around/near	70
towards/away	72

heavy/light	74
jerky/smooth	76
twisted/curled	78
boundary/along	80
beside/beyond	82
Section two: developmental motor movements	**85**
Concept games	87
Letter grids	90
Number grids	91
Body awareness	93
Tactile stimulation	96
Dominance	98
Isometrics	100
Alphabet images	102
Gross motor – locomotor activities	103
Non-locomotor activities	109
Bouncing sequences	114
Fine motor activities	117
Wrist exercises	122
Hand and finger exercises	123
Finger plays and action games	125
Finger dexterity activities	129
Cutting activities	131
Pre-writing activities	132
Drawing activities	133
Playing commercial games	134

Introduction

The concept of learning language through movement is nothing new. Piaget, Seguin, Durie and Hobb were proponents in the early 1900s.

Over many decades, educators have incorporated it into their programs. They have variously called it: reading readiness, perceptual motor programs (PMP), or sensory activities. Learning language through movement is an integral part of English as a second language (ESL) and reading intervention programs, and the core of teaching methodology for children with language delays or intellectual disorders.

What is new about this book is that it organises movement into language learning activities not only for specific target groups, but for all children.

Children progress and develop at different rates. All children learn best when we provide visual, auditory and kinasthetic supports.

No skill operates in a vacuum. Language and movement interact: movement gives vitality and form to language, and language gives understanding to movement.

Teaching children who are efficient in visual and auditory perception is well catered for in the modern curriculum. *Learning Language Through Movement* is a resource to help educators, teachers and education support staff, for children in early years settings or the foundation years of primary school.

This approach should not replace existing methodology, but add to and enhance it. The premise is that the practical games, exercises and activities add to your current classroom lessons and plans.

Section one contains movement activities to enable children to learn single-word concepts and simple phrases related to physical movement. This particularly helps those children who learn mainly through the kinaesthetic medium. The activities formalise the understanding of these words and concepts for all learners. Each pair of concepts can be used as a self contained 20 minute lesson of movement, which could be followed by the suggested classroom activities.

Section two contains information on a variety of developmental motor movements to consider and try in your setting. It includes games, exercises and activities that help develop the physical processes needed in learning language in all mediums. Again, these activities and exercises can be used in the classroom or the specialist learning setting.

Section one
Single-word concepts

This section contains individual and classroom movement activities to enable children to learn single-word concepts and simple phrases related to physical movement. The activities help children formalise a deeper understanding of these words and concepts.

Individual words/concepts are presented in opposites; a methodology that has been found to be very successful.

Here are activities that involve the whole child. Initially introduced through the kinaesthetic, they are then consolidated through the auditory and visual. This helps the child to grasp the meaning of words and concepts to which they previously may have had little or no understanding.

Words and concepts can be offered to the children verbally and visually (flashcards or whiteboard). Then the understanding is enhanced by movement activities that 'act out' the word. Flashcards are included or can be downloaded from https://bit.ly/3NJcCYT

The children say the word while they act out the meaning and work together to complete the activities. As well as language gain, this technique develops a child's receptive language and comprehension. In turn, better listening and speaking help other classroom processes.

Throughout all the large movement (gross motor) activities there should be continuous discussion. Such verbal instructions and interaction help the children understand the relationships between the concept, the word itself and the meaning.

Initially taken in an area that allows large movement (large indoor space or outdoors) these words and concepts can then be consolidated in the classroom activities. These classroom activities can be used by the teacher for the whole class or used by learning support as one-on-one activities. These activities will help children deepen their use and understanding of the words learned.

start

Equipment:

One ball per child.

Movement activities:

Children start a movement (walk, run, gallop) when the teacher says 'change', they do a different movement.

Start bouncing a ball when a teacher says 'begin'.

Always start the lesson with the children in a line – explain this is the 'start'.

Start a sequence of three balances with a wide balance.

Plan a running race with the starting procedure of: ready – set – go!

stop

Equipment:

One ball per child.

Movement activities:

Children run and stop on the teacher's signal.

Walk down the netball court and stop at the first line.

Use a wall to stop a ball when thrown.

Stop a ball rolled by a partner.

Children move around the working area, stopping and starting at the teacher's signal.

Classroom activities:

A game of 'Simon says' concentrating on start and stop.

Children form a line at the door – starting with the tallest/shortest.

Start counting by ones and stop on the teacher's signal.

Use an upper case letter to start a sentence.

Use the word 'stop' in a sentence.

Flashcards:

start

stop

up

Equipment:

Benches. One of each – beanbag, tennis bat, tennis ball and large ball for each child.

Movement activities:

Jump up into the air.

Jump up onto a bench.

Throw a beanbag up over your head.

Hit a ball repeatedly against the wall, so that each contact is higher up the wall.

Kick a ball up so it goes higher than your partner's head.

down

Equipment:

Benches. Tumbling mats. One ball per child.

Movement activities:

Step down from a bench.

Stand up, sit down.

Throw a ball down, so that it bounces before it hits a wall.

Roll down a tumbling mat.

Bounce a ball down to a partner.

Classroom activities:

Sit down on the mat on the floor.

Lift up the lid of the treasure box to see inside.

Pick up the blue crayon (various colours can be used).

Put your pencils/equipment down – various equipment can be used.

Flashcards:

up

down

above

Equipment:
Lines or ropes. One beanbag and one ball per child.

Movement activities:
Make a wide shape with both feet higher than the hands.

Catch a beanbag with both hands above the head.

Throw a ball above a line/rope.

Stand above a partner.

Make a wide shape joined to a partner, with both knees higher than your head.

below

Equipment:
One beanbag and one ball per child.

Movement activities:
Make a twisted shape with the head below the toes.

Catch a beanbag with both hands below the chin.

Bounce a ball keeping it below tummy level.

Lie below a partner.

Join with a partner to make a curled shape with your hands below the knees.

Classroom activities:

Teacher and children touch objects above or below the windows, boards, ledges etc.

Write a sentence above/below a picture.

Pin a picture on the board above/below the others.

Write the number of objects below each diagram.

What are other words that mean above/below?

Flashcards:

above

below

right

Equipment:

One hoop per child.

Movement activities:

Hop on your right foot.

Make a shape with your right hand and right foot both touching the ground.

Roll a hoop using your right hand.

Run/jump/hop/skip/gallop to the right.

left

Equipment:

One ball per child.

Movement activities:

Touch your left foot with your left hand.

Join left hands with your partner.

Bounce a ball using your left hand.

Make a shape, using your whole body (wide, thin, curled), with your left foot in the air.

Classroom activities:

Stand on the left side/right side of the classroom.

How many counters are needed to make a line across the table? Start on the left side and finish on the right.

Start your writing on the left side of the page.

Find examples of other languages that words run from right to left on a page.

Flashcards:

> right

> left

top

Equipment:
One beanbag per child.

Movement activities:
Pat your hands on top of your head.

Stand on top of the step/gutter.

Walk with a beanbag on top of your shoulder.

Lie on top of the mat.

bottom

Equipment:
One beanbag per child.

Movement activities:
Put one hand at/on the bottom of one foot.

Take the bottom beanbag from the pile.

Touch the bottom of the goal post.

Run to the bottom of the area.

Classroom activities:

Put the red block at the bottom of the pile.

Cut the top/bottom part off.

Make another word from the letters in 'top'.

Put the red block on top of two others.

Take paper from the top of the pile.

Get the story book from the top/bottom shelf.

Flashcards:

top

bottom

forward

Equipment:

Appropriate music. One bean bag and one ball per child.

Movement activities:

Walk, run and skip forward.

Throw a beanbag forward.

Bend/lean forward.

Join hands with a partner. Teacher leads locomotor movements forward in time to music.

backward

Equipment:

Appropriate music. One ball per child.

Movement activities:

Walk, hop and gallop backward.

Roll a ball backward.

Bounce a ball while moving backward.

Move backward while on all fours.

Locomotor movements backward in time to music.

Classroom activities:

Make a paper/play dough tower that leans forward or backward.

Pass the objects forward/backward.

Come forward so that you can see better.

Count forward/backward from …

Spell words forward/backward e.g. cat/dog.

Flashcards:

> forward

> backward

inside

Equipment:

One hoop and one ball per child.

Movement activities:

Stand inside the hoop.

Make a wide shape, using your whole body, with one hand and one foot inside the hoop.

Bounce a ball twice inside the hoop.

Move the hoop along the ground, staying completely inside it.

outside

Equipment:

One hoop and one ball per child.

Movement activities:

Stand outside the hoop.

Make a thin shape, with hands inside and feet outside the hoop.

Bounce a ball twice inside the hoop then twice outside the hoop.

Run around the area outside the netball court.

Classroom activities:

Place three discs or beanbags inside a circle.

Sort the objects by putting them inside different circles.

Look inside the treasure box.

Draw a circle, then place three items inside this circle and four outside it.

Using a Venn diagram – which object must stay outside all the circles?

Pack up, ready to go outside.

Flashcards:

inside

outside

before

Equipment:

One ball per child.

Movement activities:

'Before we go outside: line up at the door!'

'Before you do three hops: do two jumps!'

Children perform a movement sequence such as: a wide shape + a curled shape + a thin shape. Then ask: 'What came before the thin shape?'

Relay – bounce a ball five times before running across the netball court.

after

Equipment:

One ball per child.

Movement activities:

'Roll a ball and walk after it!'

'After you have done two jumps: do three hops!'

Children perform a movement sequence such as: two jumps + three hops + four skips + two gallops. Then ask: 'What came after the four skips?'

The teacher bounces a ball three times. Then asks: 'Bounce your ball the number of times that comes after three!'

Classroom activities:

Partner activities – one person goes before the other; then change positions.

What number comes before/after …?

Drama activities such as: the space shuttle blasts off after a countdown; the sprinter runs after the starting gun fires.

What letter of the alphabet comes before/after …?

What happened in the story before/after …?

Flashcards:

> **before**

> **after**

same

Equipment:

One ball per child. Two beanbags per child.

Movement activities:

Partners – 'Make the same shape as your partner!'

Partners – 'Bounce the ball the same as your partner!'

Partners – 'Move the same as your partner!'

Throw beanbags, one in each hand, at exactly the same time.

different

Equipment:

One ball per child.

Movement activities:

Children move around the basketball court: on a signal they must change to a different way of moving.

Partners – one child does a balance: then the partner has to do a different balance.

Partners – one child bounces a ball twice: then the partner bounces a different amount.

Standing in a circle: one at a time, children go into the middle and do a different movement.

Classroom activities:

Children put blocks into groups of the same colour.

Sort objects into criteria e.g. the same size or shape.

Write the same number in words.

List words that sound the same but look different (homophones).

Make a clump of blocks, with only one in the group being a different colour.

Solve a problem in a different way.

Visual discrimination – which one is different?

Flashcards:

> **same**

> **different**

to

Equipment:
One hoop, one beanbag and one ball per child.

Movement activities:
Walk, run, skip, to the end of the netball court.

Point to – north, the office, the canteen and other school yard landmarks.

Roll a hoop to the gutter.

Roll/throw a ball to the wall.

Throw a beanbag to a partner.

from

Equipment:
One ball per child.

Movement activities:
Walk/run/gallop from one line to another.

Face away from the teacher.

Hop from the side of the room to the first line.

Roll a ball from yourself, then go and fetch it.

Run away from a partner, then walk back to them.

Classroom activities:

Draw a line from one side of the page to the other.

Find a way through the maze from the start to the finish.

Give finished work to one person in the class.

Collect the equipment from a specific student in the class.

Count by twos from … to …

Flashcards:

to

from

front

Equipment:
One hoop and one ball per child.

Movement activities:
Hold your hoop in front of your body.

Gallop around, keeping your left foot in front of your right.

Stand in front of your partner (take turns).

Walk around bouncing a ball in front of yourself.

behind

Equipment:
One ball per child.

Movement activities:
Put your hands behind your back.

Move around keeping your left foot behind your right foot.

Follow your partner around the netball court, always keeping behind them.

Roll a ball behind yourself.

Classroom activities:

Put a red block in front of a blue one.

What is on the front cover of the book.

Come to the front of the class to share an idea.

Put a red block behind a green one.

Line up behind leaders.

Put cards in front/behind the others.

Flashcards:

front

behind

on

Equipment:

One beanbag per child.

Movement activities:

Put your hands on your chest.

Stand on a beanbag.

Walk on a white line.

Sit on the floor.

under

Equipment:

One beanbag and one ball per child.

Movement activities:

Put your fingers under your shoes.

Stand under the covered area.

Place a beanbag under a ball.

Walk under a basketball goal ring.

Classroom activities:

Put a red block on a yellow one – put the blue block under the green one.

Put finished work on the table.

Put library books back on the shelves.

Put the flashcards of all the single words covered so far into a circle – the children have to find the correct word when asked.

Rule a line under your work.

Put the words on and under into a sentence.

Flashcards:

on

under

over

Equipment:

One hoop per child.

Movement activities:

Stand over a line.

Hold your hands over your toes.

Make a shape over a hoop.

Jump over your partner.

next to

Equipment:

One hoop per child. Chalked shapes on the ground.

Movement activities:

Each girl stands next to a boy – then vice versa.

Hoops are scattered on the ground: the children run around the area, and at the signal, stand next to a hoop.

Shapes are drawn on the ground: at command the children stand next to a designated shape – wide, thin, round, twisted and so on.

Children run freely around the area: at the signal, they stand next to their partner.

Classroom activities:

Paste some blue paper over a long shape.

Children study a group of objects. The teacher then puts a towel over these objects and the children try and remember them.

Put a blue block next to a yellow one.

What numbers are next to …? What letters are next to …?

Draw a tree next to a man.

Flashcards:

over

next to

thin

Equipment:
Tumbling mats.

Movement activities:
Make your body into a thin shape.

Make a thin and low shape.

Move along the floor on your back, keeping your arms in a thin shape.

wide

Equipment:
One hoop per child.

Movement activities:
Hold your arms out wide.

Jump into the air making a wide shape.

Make a wide shape around a hoop.

Do the same wide shape as your partner (matching).

Classroom activities:

Use rods to make a thin or a wide shape.

Fold a piece of paper so that it will be thin.

Choose a book with a thin spine.

Draw pictures of animals with their legs spread wide.

List things that would be too wide to fit through the classroom door.

Spread your fingers wide to trace around them.

Flashcards:

thin

wide

big

Equipment:

One tennis ball per child.

Movement activities:

Make yourself as big as you can.

Do a series of big jumps.

Do a big bounce with a tennis ball.

Make a big wide body shape.

Mime big animal movements such as: horse, elephant and whale.

small

Equipment:

Tumbling mats. Basketballs.

Movement activities:

Move along a tumbling mat using little hops.

Do a series of small bounces with a basketball.

Make yourself as small as you can.

Make a small curled shape with four supports.

Do small non-locomotor movements such as: clicks, snaps, foot taps, wiggles.

Classroom activities:

Draw small and big pictures.

Use big letters to write your name on the board.

Draw a big object with small objects next to it.

Read a big book to the class.

Children are encouraged to take a little book home to read.

Talk about other words with the similar meanings e.g. large, little, tiny, huge.

Flashcards:

big

small

high

Equipment:

One beanbag per child.

Movement activities:

Hold your hands high above your head.

Hold your foot higher than your head.

Throw a beanbag as high as you can.

Hit a ball high into the air.

Make yourself higher than your partner.

low

Equipment:

One ball per child.

Movement activities:

Make a balance low to the ground.

Move along keeping low.

Roll a ball low towards a wall.

Throw a ball low to a partner.

Take it in turns to make a wide body shape – the same as your partner, but lower.

Classroom activities:

A game of 'Simon says' concentrating on high and low non-locomotor movements.

How high can blocks be stacked before they fall?

Work at the high/low tables.

Sit on the high/low chairs.

Discuss and role play – staying low in a smoke-filled room.

Turn the sound of music down low.

Flashcards:

> **high**

> **low**

hard

Equipment:

One bat and one tennis ball per child.

Movement activities:

Pretend to dig in hard ground.

Clap hands hard.

Hit a ball hard against a wall.

Throw a ball as hard as possible.

Push hard against a partner.

soft

Equipment:

One bat and one tennis ball per child.

Movement activities:

Pretend to softly pat a puppy.

Soft body percussion.

Make your arm muscle soft.

Hit a ball softly towards a wall.

Throw a ball softly to a partner.

Classroom activities:

Classify and group hard/soft objects.

Discuss necessity to wear bike helmets … hard ground/soft brain.

Share time with pets and baby animals – touch softly.

Press hard with a pencil to make a dark line on the page.

Discuss actions that need you to press hard or soft.

Flashcards:

hard

soft

slow

Equipment:

Music and player. Tumbling mats.

Movement activities:

Walk slowly across the basketball court.

Clap in time to slow music.

Move slowly from a curled body shape to a wide shape.

Roll slowly along a tumbling mat.

With a partner, mirror/follow the leader in a slow movement sequences, like curled balance, thin body shape, wide shape.

fast

Equipment:

Music and player. One tennis ball per child.

Movement activities:

Run fast staying inside the basketball court.

Clap hands on knees in time to fast music.

Do a fast change from a thin whole body shape to a curled one.

Throw a ball fast against a wall.

Compare moving slow and fast while walking, running, hopping and skipping.

Classroom activities:

Skip count slowly by twos.

Group a selection of animals into fast and slow moving.

Drama – act out movements and stories in slow motion.

Fast forward the audio or video recording.

Pack up fast to go to lunch.

Flashcards:

slow

fast

begin

Equipment:

Tumbling mats.

Movement activities:

From the edge of the basketball court: run to the other end and back to the beginning.

'Begin by … rolling along the mat then …'

Begin a lap of the oval slowly, so that you don't get tired near the end.

Practice the beginning of a running race: ready – set – go!

end

Equipment:

One ball per child.

Movement activities:

Run to the other end of the netball court.

Children are in lines: after they throw a ball at a wall, they go to the end of the line.

Make a sequence of three body shapes, ending in a sitting position.

End a ball-bouncing pattern by putting the ball between your feet.

The end of the race is the finish line.

Classroom activities:

Discuss similar words like start and finish.

Open a book at the beginning of a story.

Begin a sentence with an upper case letter.

End every sentence with a full stop.

Begin counting from … and end at …

Thread beads – starting with a blue one and ending with a red one.

Flashcards:

begin

end

once

Equipment:
One ball per child.

Movement activities:
Once the teacher has signalled the children are free to move.

Walk around the perimeter of the netball court once.

Jump once, hop twice, then leap once, to make a sequence.

Bounce a ball once.

Once you have bounced a ball six times, sit down.

again

Equipment:
One ball per child.

Movement activities:
Clap once, then clap again. How many is that? Clap once, then again, and again, and again, how many is that?

After you have walked across the room and back: do it again.

Roll a ball – chase and stop it; then do it again.

Complete a sequence of: one jump + one roll + one balance, then repeat.

Demonstrate a balance sequence to your partner: then your partner repeats it.

Classroom activities:

Discuss other similar words like one and repeat.

Write a row of letters once. Then write a different row of letters once and repeat them again on another line.

Fold a piece of paper once.

Make a pattern with coloured tiles – have a partner repeat the pattern.

Vote only once for your favourite book.

Flashcards:

once

again

first

Equipment:

Music and player.

Movement activities:

Run down the netball court, stopping on the first line.

Do a sequence of: three hops, three skips and three jumps; putting the jumps first.

In a race describe who comes first.

Clap in time to the music, accenting (loud clap) the first beat in a bar – (1) 2 3 4, (1) 2 3 4, (1) 2 3 4.

In groups of four, line up with the tallest first to the shortest last.

last

Equipment:

One ball per child.

Movement activities:

Do a sequence of three snaps, three clicks and three pats, with the snaps last.

Teacher repeats a sequence of body percussion (clapping body parts): name what is last in the sequence.

In groups of four: ball handling activities, taking it in turns to go last.

In groups of four: line up with the shortest last.

Classroom activities:

Which letter of the alphabet comes first? Last?

To make/bake – what is done first?

Using sequenced story card – which one comes first/last?

Verbally – which numeral comes first/last in the number…?

Draw a picture on the first page of an exercise book.

Flashcards:

first

last

second

Equipment:

Music and player.

Movement activities:

Walk the length of the netball court, stopping at the second line.

Movement sequence of body shapes: wide balance, twisted shape, curled shape, thin shape. Which shape was second?

Clap in time to the music: accenting (louder) every second beat.

Races involving six to eight children running, hopping, or skipping. The other children must judge who finishes second.

third

Equipment:

None.

Movement activities:

Walk the length of the netball court, jumping after every third step.

Children line up in groups of five. Who is the third tallest in each group?

Children do a movement sequence with the third movement being a wide balance.

Six children at a time have races (running, hopping, galloping); the other children decide who finishes third.

Classroom activities:

Put the red block second in a line of five.

What is the second/third letter of a particular word?

Skip counting by twos from ... Which number comes second?

Make a line of discs: the third one along has to be a double-decker (two-high).

What was the second/third activity in a sequence?

In the Olympics, what colours are the second and third place medallions?

Flashcards:

second

third

whole

Equipment:

Benches and tumbling mats.

Movement activities:

Lie your whole body on a bench.

Run along the whole boundary of the basketball court.

Make your whole body roll over.

Shake your whole body at once.

part

Equipment:

One beanbag per child. Tumbling mats.

Movement activities:

Shake one part of your body.

Make a wide shape with four body parts touching the ground.

Throw a beanbag part way to a line.

Roll over part way and back again.

Classroom activities:

Put discs around a whole circle.

Complete the whole puzzle.

Put discs part way around a circle.

Where will this part of the jigsaw puzzle go?

Cut the whole cake into two parts and then eat one part.

In book discussion – children talk about their favourite part of the story.

Flashcards:

whole

part

all

Equipment:
One ball per child.

Movement activities:
Walk along all/every line in the netball court.

All the children together move around the netball court.

Every time you take a step you bounce the ball.

All children to bounce the ball at the same time.

half

Equipment:
One ball per child.

Movement activities:
Make yourself only half as high as you really are.

Jump, turning halfway around (180 degrees) in the air.

Run halfway down the basketball court, and back again.

Partners – bounce a ball half as many times as a partner.

Split children into half – two groups.

Classroom activities:

Join all the dots between the numbers ... to ...

Complete all the questions on the page.

Make a list of all the things that happen every day

Divide a circle in half.

How many jellybeans will you get if you divide them in half?

Flashcards:

| **all** |

| **half** |

more

Equipment:

One ball and one hoop per child.

Movement activities:

The teacher throws a ball into the air and catches it, the children do the same action but more times.

Bounce a ball more times in a hoop than a partner.

Circle a hoop with one arm six times. Then circle it more than six times with the other arm.

Throw a ball into the air and catch it six times using both hands. Then throw the ball up and catch it more than six times using one hand only.

less

Equipment:

None.

Movement activities:

One partner skips across the netball court, then the other does it in less skips.

One partner does six kangaroo (double fast) jumps. The other partner has to do one less.

One partner takes six big steps backward, then the other partner takes six steps forward in the same direction. Which of the two takes/makes the less distance?

In groups of four – make a combined wide shape with less than eight supports.

Classroom activities:

Put more or less numbers of blocks in piles.

Count partner's blocks to see who has the more or less.

What number is two more/less than …?

Which object weighs more/less?

Flashcards:

| **more** |

| **less** |

almost

Equipment:
One ball per child.

Movement activities:
Run almost to the end of the court and back.

Make yourself almost as small as you can. Can you get any smaller?

Throw the ball almost as high as the roof.

Make yourself almost as tall as your partner.

as many

Equipment:
One tambourine.

Movement activities:
The teacher taps the tambourine five times; children respond with five claps.

Walk across the area, taking as many steps as you can to get there.

Partners: do as many jumps/hops/kicks as the leader.

Classroom activities:

Draw a line across the page so that it almost reaches the other edge.

Pour water into the container until it is almost full.

Build a single block tower – almost as tall as your partners.

Using blocks, build a single block tower; using as many blocks as possible before it falls over.

Fit as many marbles/beads into a jar as you can – then count them.

Write as many correct words as you can in one minute.

Flashcards:

almost

as many

corner

Equipment:

Hand-drawn metre squares. One beanbag per child.

Movement activities:

Stand in the corner of the netball court.

In a metre square, balance so that a hand or foot is in each corner.

Children throw a beanbag to land in the corner of a metre square.

Children run around inside the netball court, and do three jumps in each of its corners.

row

Equipment:

Four beanbags per child. Lots of hoops.

Movement activities:

Children stand in rows organised by the teacher.

Children have free play with their four beanbags: on a signal they arrange them in rows.

Teacher calls a number two to four, and the children arrange the beanbags in rows of this number.

Children have four beanbags each. In turn they throw them into a line/row of four hoops nearest to furthest.

Classroom activities:

Write your name in the corner of any completed work.

Quietly reading in the library corner.

Place blocks in rows of given numbers.

What number in this row is missing?

Measure the length of a row of toy cars.

Flashcards:

corner

row

with

Equipment:

One hoop per child. Tumbling mats.

Movement activities:

Move across the room with a marching action.

Cross a tumbling mat with a series of hops.

With a hoop: make a wide shape.

Stand with a partner.

With your partner make a twisted shape/balance that has a total of seven supports.

at

Equipment:

One tennis ball per child. A soccer ball and skittles per group.

Movement activities:

Stand at the centre of the basketball court.

At the teacher's command, move as requested: walk, run, skip, gallop.

Throw a tennis ball at a target.

Roll a soccer ball at some skittles.

Sit at your partners feet.

Classroom activities:

Draw different animals with different designated pencils.

Point to the words with a finger when you are reading.

Fill in each shape with a different colour.

Look at different objects, as nominated by the teacher.

Look at the illustration for a clue to this new word.

Wait at the red door after lunch.

Flashcards:

with

at

across

Equipment:

Tumbling mats. One ball and one hoop per child.

Movement activities:

Walk backwards across a netball court.

Jump across a hoop.

Roll across a tumbling mat.

Throw a ball across a gym.

Alternately move across a partner's legs.

diagonal

Equipment:

Tumbling mats. A piece of chalk and one ball per child.

Movement activities:

Walk diagonally across the room.

Draw a diagonal line across the netball court.

Roll a ball in a diagonal across a netball third.

Make a diagonal shape with your arms.

Move around, then across, then diagonally over a tumbling mat.

Classroom activities:

Rule lines across a page.

Draw a line across a page to join a picture to its matching word.

Draw vertical, horizontal and diagonal lines.

Which line(s) of a triangle are diagonal?

Fold a square in half along its diagonal.

X is made by drawing two diagonal lines.

Flashcards:

> # across

> # diagonal

straight

Equipment:

Tumbling mats. One ball and one cone per child.

Movement activities:

Walk, run, skip, gallop along a straight line.

Walk along keeping arms/legs straight.

Roll along a tumbling mat keeping both legs straight.

Roll a ball in a straight line to hit a marker.

curved

Equipment:

One ball per child.

Movement activities:

Make a curved shape using both your arms and legs.

Walk/skip/hop along a curved line.

Bounce a ball while you are moving in a curved line.

Try and roll/spin a ball, to move in a curved motion.

Mirror a partner's curved shape.

Classroom activities:

Drawing straight and curved lines.

Name three things in the room that have straight/curved lines.

Cut straight along the line.

Which letters in the alphabet have only straight/curved lines?

Draw a robot using only straight/curved lines?

Make the picture on the wall hang straight.

Flashcards:

straight

curved

match

Equipment:

Music and player.

Movement activities:

Matching is doing the same thing as your partner: either alongside or after them (follow the leader).

Match your partners height.

Match your partners movement sequence: such as – run – run – run – jump.

Match your partner's dance step.

mirror

Equipment:

One ball per child.

Movement activities:

Mirroring is doing the same thing as your partner while facing them (like looking in a mirror).

Mirror a partner's movements – take it in turn to choose.

Mirror a curled shape with four supports.

Mirror a partner bouncing a ball.

Mirror in a group of four – an upside down shape with five supports.

Classroom activities:

Place Lego blocks in matching and mirroring positions.

Children match different shapes with their partner.

Match the word with its picture/number.

Jumble the shoes and then match them again.

Draw the other half of a picture as though it can be seen in a mirror.

Draw a mirror image if the mirror was held at the side and then at the bottom.

Flashcards:

match

mirror

through

Equipment:
Eight long ropes. One beanbag and one hoop per child.

Movement activities:
Walk through a shape made by ropes on the ground.

Throw a beanbag through a hoop held by your partner.

Pass your whole body through a hoop while holding it with one hand.

Run through a rope being turned by two others.

between

Equipment:
Markers/witches hats. One beanbag per child.

Movement activities:
Move (locomotor movements – walk, hop, run, skip, gallop) keeping between the markers.

Make a curled shape and keep your hands between your feet.

Move around the area – walk, jump, crawl – keeping a beanbag between your feet.

Crawl between your partners legs.

Classroom activities:

Passing beads through a circle.

Push the thread through the letter beads to spell a word.

Push the pin through the paper to make a shape/letter/number.

Place a red block between two yellow ones.

Which number comes between five and seven?

When you write, you hold the pencil between your thumb and forefinger.

Flashcards:

> # through

> # between

side

Equipment:

One hoop per child.

Movement activities:

Hold a hoop to the side of your body.

Jump to the side.

Rock from side to side.

Run/skip/hop/gallop to the side of the netball court.

middle

Equipment:

One hoop and one ball per child.

Movement activities:

Hop in the middle of your hoop.

Run and jump to land in the middle of your hoop.

Bounce a ball in the middle of your hoop.

Children are numbered in pairs. On signal, each pair has to run to the middle of the basketball court.

Classroom activities:

Draw circles on one side of the page.

Draw a picture on one side of a line and its matching word on the other side.

Start reading and writing from the left side of the page.

Draw triangles in the middle of the page.

Which number is in the middle of this row?

Which letter is in the middle of these three letter words?

What is the middle sound of this word?

Flashcards:

side

middle

around

Equipment:

One hoop and one ball per child.

Movement activities:

Hop around your hoop.

Walk/run/skip around the outside of the netball court.

Spin around like a top.

Pat bounce (dribble) a ball around a partner.

near

Equipment:

Markers/witches hats. One beanbag per child.

Movement activities:

Stand near a line.

Roll a ball so that it keeps near to the line.

Make a curled shape, with your head near one knee.

Run/skip/gallop staying near/close to your partner.

Classroom activities:

Put an elastic band around your work to take it home.

Draw a circle around the numbers that are close to 10.

Place a green block near/close to a yellow one.

'Why will our classroom plants grow better closer to the window?'

Find the contents page near the front of the book.

Flashcards:

around

near

towards

Equipment:
One ball and one marker cone for each pair.

Movement activities:
Hold one hand in front of your body – move the other hand towards it.

Run/hop/skip/gallop towards a line.

Roll a ball towards a marker cone.

Jump towards a partner.

away

Equipment:
Tumbling mats. One ball per child.

Movement activities:
Roll a ball away from yourself, then run to stop it.

Pat bounce a ball, keeping it as far away from your body as possible.

Roll along a tumbling mat, keeping your hands away from your feet.

Skip away from a partner and then back again.

Classroom activities:

Roll a bead towards the side of your table.

Roll dice towards the wall so that they don't fall off the table.

Read the instructions of the board game – the markers move towards the finish and away from the start.

Start with two blocks: move them away from each other.

Remember these five objects – which one has been taken away?

Flashcards:

towards

away

heavy

Equipment:

None.

Movement activities:

Children pretend to be Olympic weightlifters lifting a heavy weight.

Children pretend to be heavy animals who have to move around.

Children pick up different items to find the heaviest one.

Children pretend to be heavy dead weights.

Practise jumping and landing heavily.

light

Equipment:

Light music and player. One ball per child.

Movement activities:

Light locomotor movements: tiptoe, run, skip.

Non-locomotor light movements: floating, flicking, gliding, waffling.

Light movements to music.

Lightly throw a ball.

Jumping and landing lightly.

Classroom activities:

Colour in geometric shapes – alternately heavy and light.

Put something heavy on the flowers to press them flat.

Estimate if objects are heavier or lighter than yourself.

Press the pencil down heavy for the outline and then light to colour in.

Ring the metal bell strongly and the glass bell lightly. Why? Discuss heavy and light.

Flashcards:

heavy

light

jerky

Equipment:
None.

Movement activities:
Children move down the netball court, stopping and starting at random.

Run/skip/hop/gallop constantly changing directions.

Non-locomotor jerky movements: flicks, taps, kicks, hits, pushes, pulls.

Locomotor jerky movements: skip, gallop, twist.

Mime jerky movements: toy soldiers, skeletons, robots.

smooth

Equipment:
Appropriate music and player.

Movement activities:
Children move down the netball court, smoothly changing directions.

A balance sequence: wide, thin, curled – with smooth changes.

Non-locomotor smooth movements – waves, balances, leaps.

Smooth locomotor and non-locomotor movements to music.

Mime smooth movements – ballerinas, car gear changes, elite runners.

Classroom activities:

Children draw a story, contrasting the opposites, such as: the ballerina and the robot, or soldiers and runners.

Make a jerky zigzag pattern across a page.

Drama – driving a jerky car or riding a jerky roller coaster.

Join loops smoothly across a page.

Track reading with a finger to help you read smoothly.

Smooth out Easter egg foils for an art activity.

Flashcards:

jerky

smooth

twisted

Equipment:
Tumbling mats.

Movement activities:
Twist arms and legs together.

Make a shape/balance that is twisted and has five supports.

Move down the basketball court in a twisted pathway.

Roll along a tumbling mat in a twisted shape.

Partner matching twisted shapes.

curled

Equipment:
Tumbling mats. Music and player.

Movement activities:
Curl fingers to make a fist.

Make a shape/balance that is curled and has three supports.

Move along a tumbling mat in a curled shape.

While holding a curled balance – clap in time to the music.

Partner matching – curled shapes.

Classroom activities:

Plaiting string, twine or cord by twisting it.

Twist the lids off jars – take a sniff and guess what's in them.

Twist bread ties around plants to hold them to the stakes.

A discussion to find synonyms for 'curled' – rolled-up, ball, squashed, round.

Curl a piece of paper around a pencil to make a curled shape.

Why do animals curl up to keep warm?

Flashcards:

> # twisted

> # curled

boundary

Equipment:

One tennis ball and one hoop per child.

Movement activities:

Walk around the outside of the netball court (the boundary).

Free play with tennis balls inside the boundary of the basketball court.

Make a curled shape using a hoop as a boundary.

Jog along the boundary line of the football ground.

Stand on the opposite side of the boundary line to your partner.

along

Equipment:

One hoop and one ball per child.

Movement activities:

Walk along the outside of the football ground.

Run along to the other end of the basketball court.

Roll a ball along using one foot.

Children bowl a hoop along beside themselves.

Pulling a partner along a tumbling mat.

Classroom activities:

Place rods/sticks/blocks along the edge of a page to form a boundary.

Name objects near to the school boundary.

On a map, draw a red line along the boundary.

How many blocks fit side by side along a ruler?

Push toy cars along marked roads on the map.

Flashcards:

boundary

along

beside

Equipment:

One beanbag per child.

Movement activities:

Stand beside the end white line of the basketball court.

Place the beanbag beside your right foot.

Throw a beanbag to land beside the wall.

Stand beside a partner.

Run down the court keeping beside a partner.

beyond

Equipment:

One ball and one beanbag per child.

Movement activities:

Walk/run/gallop to stop beyond a line.

Roll a ball to stop beyond a marker.

Throw a beanbag to land beyond a line.

Hit a ball beyond a cricket pitch.

Move in a straight line to stop beyond your partner, taking it in turns to move.

Classroom activities:

Place the same coloured blocks beside each other.

Write the corresponding word beside the picture.

Which two letters are beside 'm' in the alphabet?

Draw a child throwing a beanbag beyond a line.

Count beyond a certain number.

Flashcards:

| beside |

| beyond |

Section two
Developmental motor movements

This section contains games, exercises and activities that help develop the physical processes needed in learning language and writing readiness. It also provides information about developmental motor movements.

There is general agreement within education and academic circles that a close relationship exists between visual, auditory and motor analysis skills. Children need to discover how their bodies move. They need to distinguish between movements of different parts of the body and to learn to adapt to the environment and integrate the use of their body as they move through space.

Body awareness and understanding of how their body moves helps to develop the perceptual skills needed in all mediums of learning. Children need to identify and recognise their own body in different surroundings and must realise the potential outcome of any intended movement.

The understanding of concepts, sequential memory work and concentration are all developed by combining language and associated physical activity.

Hand-eye coordination, fine motor and gross motor development, enhance analytical ability by enabling the child to complete different tasks. These skills and perceptions then assist the visual mechanisms involved in literacy and numeracy.

Children develop two types of motor (movement) skills: 'fine' motor skills and 'gross' motor skills. Fine motor skills involve using hands and fingers to control smaller objects. Gross motor skills involve the coordination of larger muscles in the body to make larger movements.

A child's awareness of available space around them for movement requires visual and auditory scanning, and minor physical adjustments prior to any major movement. The more refined this preparation for movement, the more efficient and controlled the movement will be. The scanning of the physical environment using visual and auditory senses is the same process used in scanning for detail in literacy and numeracy.

Topics covered in this section include body awareness, fine motor and gross motor activities, balance and bouncing exercises, finger and wrist exercises and more.

Concept games

Games are an essential part of the learning process. They help children bond with others, burn off excess energy and teach them skills that will support them later in life. Concept games teach children different skills, ideas, thoughts and perceptions. Concept games also encourage great engagement and language opportunities for many children.

Big A – little A

Children line up at one end of the netball court or room. One child is selected as the 'cat' and then stands at the other end to the rest, and with their back towards them.

The children chant: 'Big A, little A, and bouncing B, the cat's in the cupboard and can't catch me!'

On 'Big A' – they all stand on tiptoe, with arms up stretched.
On 'Little A' – they crouch as low as possible.
On 'Bouncing B' – they advance three steps towards the 'cat'.
On 'The cat's in the cupboard and can't catch me!', they advance on tiptoe.

When someone is close enough, on the word 'me', they tag the 'cat', who then tries to catch as many of them as possible before they can get back to the line.

Magic ring

The children stand in a single circle. One person is selected as the 'witch', and stands in the middle of this circle with a wand.

Using this wand, the 'witch' directs the rest to do certain activities, such as: hop, jump, wave, sit down.

When the 'witch' breaks the spell by dropping the wand, she chases the rest of the children, trying to tag as many as possible.

What's the time Mr Wolf?

The children line up at one end of the area. The child selected as the 'wolf', stands at the other end with their back to the group.

The children advance towards the 'wolf' chanting: 'What's the time Mr. Wolf?'

Mr. Wolf turns and says 'Three o'clock!' Where upon the children jump three times (if ten o'clock, there would be ten jumps).

This continues until the 'wolf' says 'Dinner time', which signals that he chases the children back to the line, tagging as many as possible.

Here – there – where

The children are in free spacing inside the court or room. The teacher calls out any of the three words in the title of the game. If 'Here', the children run towards the teacher. If 'There', they run towards where the teacher points. If 'Where', they perform a designated activity on the spot. This 'Where' activity is decided upon beforehand, such as: a balance, a hop or running on the spot.

Do this – do that

The children face the leader. This leader performs any movements, at the same time saying 'Do this!' All the players copy this action.

If the leader says 'Do that', and a player copies the action, then they are out of the game, or must pay a forfeit (such as a jog around the netball court).

Doctor tag

If tagged by the player who is 'it': the player who has been tagged, must hold the part of their body where they were touched. Then with this handicap, they chase the others.

Rabbits in burrows

The class is divided into threes, and then put into a single circle. All facing the centre of the circle, two children join hands to form the burrow, and the third squats down under these hands, to be a rabbit in the burrow.

There are two odd players, one who is a 'rabbit', and another who is a 'dog'. The 'dog' chases the 'rabbit', which can enter 'burrow' from the back, which means that a new 'rabbit' must run out through the front to be chased. If/when a 'rabbit' is tagged, both 'dog' and 'rabbit' become 'burrows'.

Potato race

Potatoes, stones, beanbags, or some other such markers, are placed in front of each team. A basket, box, bucket, or some other appropriate container is placed at the head of each line.

These markers may be picked up in any order.

Number 1 in each team runs to one marker, picks it up, and returns it to the basket; then goes back and picks up the next, and so on until all their team's markers are in their team's container.

Then Number 2 replaces the markers on their spots again, one at a time. Number 3 picks them up, and Number 4 replaces them again, and so on.

The first team finished is the winner.

Ducklings fly

All players face the leader. The leader calls out an activity that is related to a specific animal: dogs – bark, horses – gallop, fish – swin. The players imitate this action.

If an action is called that is inappropriate to the animal such as: cats – bark, ducklings – fly, the players should not imitate this action. If an inappropriate action is done by a player, a forfeit must be paid.

Letter grids

There are a variety of activities you can do with a letter grid. It is suggested that the grid is created for children in chalk outside so they have room to move and participate. Children can work in pairs or individually on the activities.

Provide children with the sounds that the letters make to support phonemic awareness.

Activities:

Step/hop/jump on the letters of their first name in order.

Step/hop/jump on the letters of their last name in order.

Step/hop/jump on the letters of the alphabet that are vowels.

Step/hop/jump on the letters of ten consonants.

Spell CVC words or high frequency words by placing a different body part on each letter of the word being spelled.

Spell the name of partner by hopping on the letters in correct order.

An example of a letter grid that could be drawn in chalk:

g	t	y	j	s	m
l	d	q		e	u
x		f	w	o	b
p	a	v	c		k
	n	r	h	z	i

Number grids

Like letter grids, number grids provide a vareity of opportunities for children. These grids can be created outside with chalk or by using numbered disc equipment.

Activities:

Step/hop/jump on each number in order from one to nine.

Step/hop/jump each number backwards from nine to one.

Step/hop/jump on different even numbers.

Step/hop/jump on different odd numbers.

Write and solve simple addition, subtraction and multiplication problems by stepping, hopping or jumping on the numbers and mathematical signs.

A variety of number grids can be created:

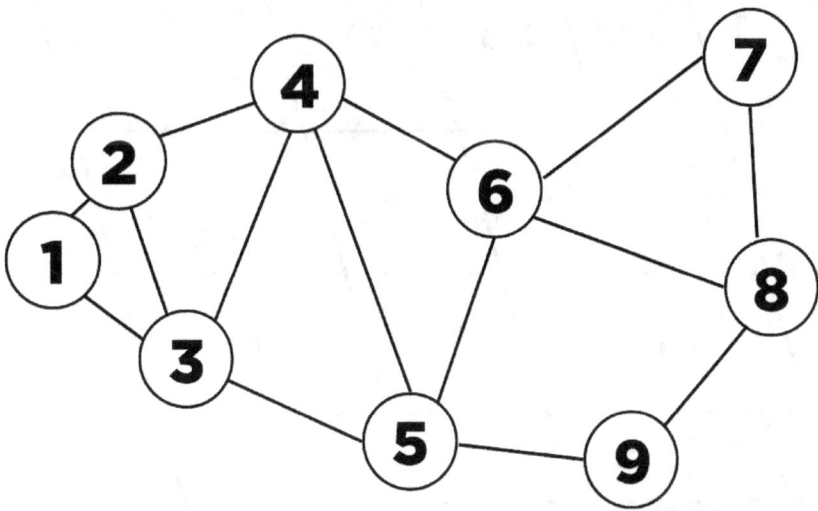

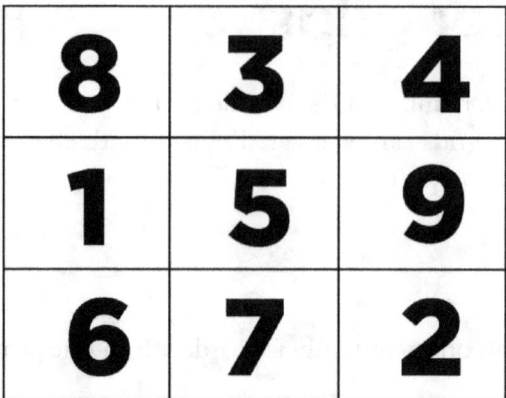
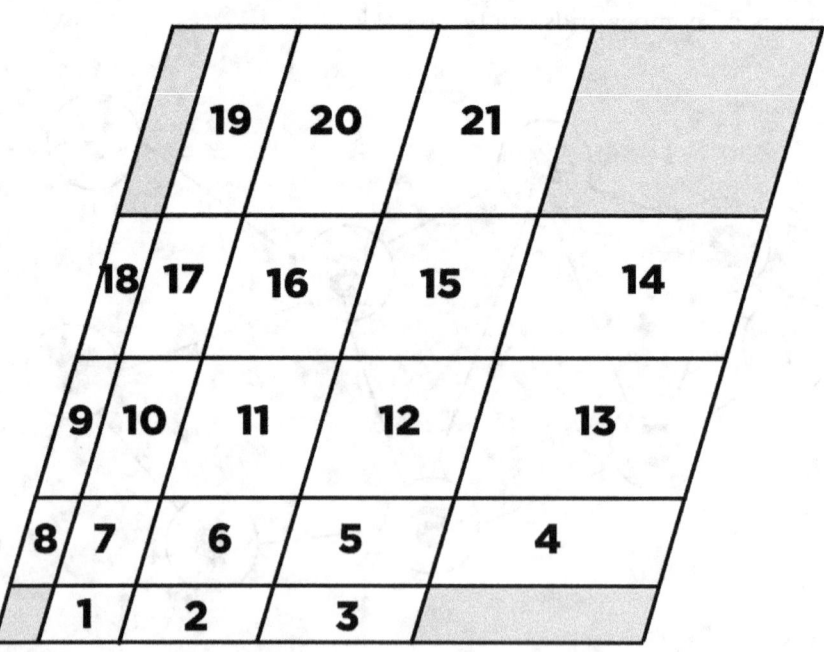

Body awareness

Body awareness is the ability to understand where our bodies are in space and how our bodies move. Body awareness activities for children help them to understand how to relate to objects and people at home, in a learning environment and outdoors. For example, properly developed body awareness tells us how far to reach for objects or how close to stand next to a person.

All children may not have the same abilities to interpret and form a motor action when it comes to body awareness. This can result in them having difficulties with personal space, following motor directions, participating in sports and more.

Activities:

Teach/revise identification and location of body planes.

Teach/revise identification and location of major and minor body parts.

Specific body parts.

Revision of specific body areas e.g.: face, trunk, leg.

Abstraction work e.g.: touching self, partners, body parts.

Locate parts of a picture, body jigsaw etc.

Incorporate balance tasks into body parts.

Children trace around each other's body parts and then swap to colour code body parts.

Mirror work – children look in mirror making themselves: small, large, wide, narrow.

Like an octopus, giraffe, elephant.

Moving fingers, hands, legs, arms.

Children stand opposite the teacher copying the touching of body parts, these are verbalised.

Touch your own legs, head to same.

This is my head, touch your head.

Create a body using equipment (hoops, blocks, beanbags). Children can walk/balance on different body parts.

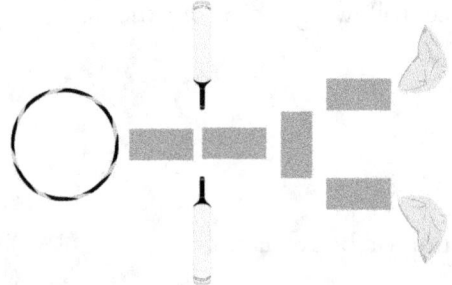

Create artwork about bodies.

Touch body parts on command.

'I spy with my little eye'. Children say and touch.

Children are shown pictures of specific body parts and are asked to identify them.

Children are blindfolded and touch own body parts.

Draw a picture of yourself.

Touch body parts to the surroundings.

Draw incomplete figure and children complete.

Touch body parts with other body parts.

Follow the leader, walking along and touching body parts as the leader calls them out.

Paper doll – children to make, then dress a paper figure.

Play 'hokey pokey'.

Tactile stimulation

Tactile learning and stimulation are essential for a child's growth in their physical abilities, cognitive and language skills, and social and emotional development.

Our touch system, comprising our skin, is sensitive and thus reactive to changes in our environment, such as detecting changes in pressure, temperature, pain, and different types of touch sensations. The receptors in our skin carry this information to the brain where the brain interprets this information and decides how to respond.

Tactile stimulation activities can be an important part of a sensory diet or fine motor skills program. Tactile activities are helpful with hand and finger awareness attention, and fine motor planning.

Activities:

Face down
Eyes open then closed with children pressing body parts against the floor

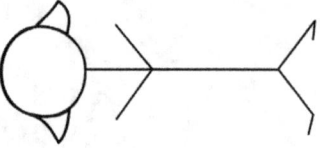

Face up
Eyes open then closed with children pressing body parts against the floor

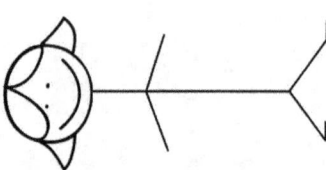

Then children bend over to press holes in the floor.

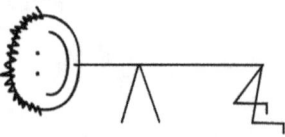

Children lean back and press with backs against walls, while pressing slide down to a sitting position as if on a chair

Lean with arms outstretched and push the wall down.

Children stand back to back. One pushes backward; the other child resists, but lets self be pushed across the room while slightly resisting.

Children face to face pressing against each other palms.

One child lies face up on the floor, eyes closed; their partner has a soft ball attached to a stick – gently touches body parts which the first child identifies by name.

Dominance

Hand dominance, hand preference or handedness are all terms used to describe a child's natural inclination for favouring one hand over the other for skill activities. These include functional activities (e.g. tooth and hair brushing) and learning tasks (e.g. handwriting and scissor skills).

The onset of hand dominance usually witnesses the non-dominant hand becoming consistently used as the supporting hand. Some children may take longer to establish hand dominance, particularly those who have had difficulty and avoided fine motor tasks earlier in their development.

Hand dominance is an important skill in child's development as it ensures proficiency and efficiency in tasks that involve more complex motor plans, motor accuracy and greater skill. An ability to cross the midline and bilaterally coordinate the hands are contributing foundation skills that ensure consistency in hand dominance (e.g. in a cutting a piece of paper, one hand needs to know that it is going to cut, while the other is going to support it by holding onto the paper).

Activities:

Right hand activities

Left hand activities

Dominant hand activities   hold
throw
small motor activities
large motor activities.

Right foot/leg activities

Left foot/leg activities

Dominant foot/leg activities   kick
jump
small movements
large movements.

Point dominant arm   parallel to floor in front
                           to back
                           quarter turn

Whole body   half turn right
                           quarter-turn
                           hop/jump

Obstacle course turning from one direction to another. Children tell other children what they have done.

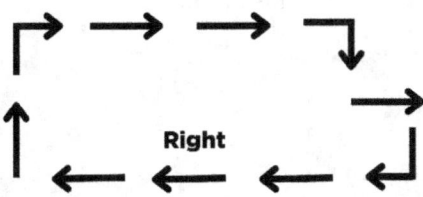

Child moves along line telling you what they see. e.g. 'There is a square on my right. I can turn right and jump over it.'

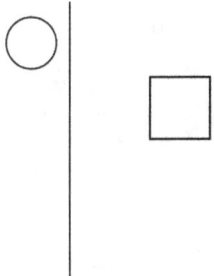

Cross directions e.g. right hand on left knee

Sequence in body parts; clap twice, put your elbows together, put your feet apart, touch your right knee with your left hand.

Isometrics

Isometric exercises are those in which a muscle tenses but doesn't contract or works harder than others. These exercises target specific muscles for strengthening. Isometric activities can normally be done either sitting or standing and without much movement or a large space.

For some children, doing isometric exercises may improve concentration and focus. If a child starts to get fidgety or their focus wanders, some isometric exercises might help before returning to task at hand.

Activities:

Children interlace fingers, press palms together

Head to side; keeping face forward for tension felt in neck; keep other parts still; head forward; feel tension in back of neck; head backwards; feel tension in front of neck.

Children sit cross legged, hands behind neck, fingers interlaced, bend forward.

Children lie face up on floor, knees slightly bent stretch arms and legs forward, raise head neck and shoulders.

Same position knees bent, feet flat. Contract abdomen.

Children sit on floor, knees bent, feet on floor (hook position.)

Shift weight backward onto lower back, letting feet rise from floor.

The children try to 'melt' into the floor while on backs face up. This exercise should be done with eyes both opened and closed. While 'melting' into the floor or during any rest period children can become aware of inner movement.

Head roll slowly.

Shoulder roll slowly.

Children sit cross legged and let body droop forward in a relaxed position.

Slowly raise knees, feet slide along floor to trunk.

Relax muscles in legs and slide down.

Alphabet images

Children can use their whole body to form lower case letters, spell out their names or create simple words as a class. Children will develop body awareness while learning about shapes and the alphabet. Provide the children with the sounds of the letters they are creating to support phonemic awareness.

Gross motor – locomotor activities

A locomotor skill is a physical action that propels an individual from one place to another. This may mean moving forward, backward or even upwards using certain skills.

These skills help to refine a child's gross motor abilities. The more often locomotor skills are practised, the greater the child's ability to fine tune the movement of each skill. For example, with sufficient practise a child who is able to hop in place becomes able to play hopscotch.

The activities start with skills that are easier to master, and then progresses to the more difficult movements, like leaping.

Activities:

Walking

Walk lightly, shoulders loose, toes pointing forward.

Walk in a circle – be careful not to touch anyone.

Walk on tiptoes, balancing carefully.

Raise arms as you tiptoe – notice how it helps you balance.

Move on your tiptoes from one place to another – walk naturally, going quickly and quietly from one place to another.

Walk one way, on signal, change direction.

Walk backwards without touching anyone.

Walk in a fun way – laughing and smiling.

Scowl and walk like you are angry.

Start walking tall.

Bend your knees and walk small.

Walk tall/low in one direction then change on signal.

Walk tall in one direction, low in another, keep changing.

Let your hands hang below your knees and walk like a gorilla.

Bend your knees as low as you can.

Walk low and hold your hands high.

Walk stepping first on your toes then heels, as fast as you can (toe-heel walk).

Walk against a strong wind – change body positions to accommodate it.

Running

Running forwards.

Running backwards.

Running sideways.

Running changing direction.

Running slowly.

Running fast.

Running change speed.

Running lifting knees high.

Running with legs straight.

Running with long strides.

Running with short strides.

Running whilst stretching.

Running whilst curling.

Running whilst twisting.

Combination of two or more running activities in a sequence.

Jumping

Jumping is a whole body exercise which is comprised of the preparation phase (bending of the knees, hips, arms swing backwards), the take off phase (arms are propelled forwards and upwards as the body pushes off from the ground) and the landing phase (the arms come down to extend in front of the body and the feet land together with knees and hips bent). This requires motor planning and sequencing skills.

Jumping from a standing position.

Jumping from a crouched position.

Jumping using a walking approach.

Jumping using a running approach.

Jumping making a wide shape in the air.

Jumping making a thin shape in the air.

Jumping making a curled shape in the air.

Jumping making a stretched shape in the air.

Jumping with a one foot take off.

Jumping with a two foot take off.

Jumping changing level.

Jumping with explosive action.

Jumping slowly.

Jumping changing speed.

Jumping forwards.

Jumping backwards.

Jumping sideways.

Jumping turning in the air.

Jumping over equipment.

Jumping onto equipment.

Jumping off equipment.

Jumping landing on two feet.

Jumping landing on one foot.

Combinations of two or more of the above into sequences.

Leaping

Leaping is a different set of skills from jumping. Leaping requires stepping or jumping forward or back with one leg outstretched; taking off on one foot and landing on the other.

Run with small steps then take a giant leap into the air.

Run again leap, thrust right leg and left arm forward.

Run again leap, reverse above.

Run forward, stop and turn around; then run back and leap as far as you can.

Bend knees and leap low. Who can leap the lowest?

Clap your hands above your head as you leap.

Reach up with both hands as you leap, as if you wanted to catch something high above your head.

Leap high and land low.

Be a giant, bounding in great leaps across the country.

Find a line, leap back and forth.

Run and leap at the teacher's signal.

Rolling

Rolling is one of first skills children learn as babies and over time their skills in rolling develops especially into crawling. As children grow they will learn to roll differently like rolling down a slope or being rolled up in a rug/blanket. Children need to learn to rotate the trunk with increasing upper body strength and body awareness to develop their rolling skills.

Rolling from a crouched position.

Rolling from a standing position.

Rolling from a lying position.

Rolling from a shoulder balance.

Rolling from a walking approach.

Rolling from a rocking approach.

Rolling in a stretched shape.

Rolling in a curled shape.

Rolling sideways.

Rolling changing direction.

Rolling fast.

Rolling slowly.

Combinations of two or more of the above.

Other locomotor movements

Other locomotor movements can be explored using activities suggested for walking and running.

These are: skipping
 galloping
 slipping
 hopping
 crawling
 animal movements.

Non-locomotor activities

Non-locomotor skills are fundamental body movements that do not incorporate travelling. They are stability skills that include movements of limbs or body parts, and sometimes even the whole body. They are occasionally referred to as axial movements, as in 'revolving around an axis'. Here, the axis is the centre portion of the child's body, or generally the child's torso. The child's 'axis' experiences little to no movement.

These movements and activities can be done in a variety of postures, including standing, sitting and lying.

Activities:

Leg movements:
bending
kicking
stretching
swinging
placing
lunging
raising
circling.

Arm movements:
bending
circling
stretching
pounding
raising
flicking
swinging
dabbing.

Trunk movements:
bending
swinging
lowering
stretching
leaning
raising
curling

spanning
turning
pressing
tensing
twisting.

Balancing

Balance is the ability to maintain a controlled body position during a task. To function effectively across environments and tasks, children need the ability to maintain controlled positions during both static (still) and dynamic (moving) activities. Static balance is the ability to hold a stationary position with control (e.g. freeze or statue games). Dynamic balance is the ability to remain balanced while engaged in movement (e.g. riding a bike).

Balancing on the feet.

Balancing on one foot.

Balancing on the knees.

Balancing on one knee.

Balancing on the seat.

Balancing on the shoulders.

Combinations of the above.

Balancing in a wide shape.

Balancing in a thin shape.

Balancing in a curled shape.

Balancing in a bridge position.

Balancing in a twisted shape.

Matching a balance performed by a partner.

Balancing with a complimentary balance.

Balancing to perform a combined partner balance.

Balancing in a group balance.

Linking a balance to another activity.

Walking on a balance beam.

Mounting a beam maintaining balance.

Balancing on a beam using hands to support body.

Rocking

Rocking, like the other movements in this section, will stimulate the vestibular system, which helps the body to know how it is moving and how fast it is moving. Depending on their intensity, vestibular activities can be stimulating or calming for some children.

Rocking whilst standing.

Rocking whilst kneeling.

Rocking whilst crouching.

Rocking whilst lying on back.

Rocking whilst lying on side.

Rocking whilst lying on front.

Rocking on hands and feet.

Rocking forwards.

Rocking backwards.

Rocking from side to side.

Rocking changing direction.

Rocking fast.

Rocking slowly.

Rocking varying speed.

Rocking in a stretched shape.

Rocking in a curled shape.

Rocking to a rhythm.

Linking rocking to other movements.

Combining two or more of the above in a combined sequence.

Weight on hands

Body weight activities stimulate proprioceptive input. These activities require children to put weight into their hands to do a vareity of things with their bodies. These body weight activities can help some children release energy, which in turn will increase their attention and focus.

Weight on hands in a wide shape.

Weight on hands in a thin shape.

Weight on hands in a curled shape.

Weight on hands changing shape.

Mountain climbers. Extend legs back and forth.

Weight on hands, elbow and knee balance.

Weight on hands – alligator balance.

Sitting on hands.

Planking. Challenge the children to who can plank the longest.

Weight on hands changing shapes.

Weight on two hands, one foot.

Weight on one hand, two feet.

Keeping hands on spot but moving on feet.

Weight on hands on equipment.

Combining two or more of the above in a sequence.

Performing any of the above to form a partner balance.

Bouncing sequences

Bouncing is different to jumping. When you jump it is done with the limbs (especially legs) working from coiled to extension to provide power to 'lift off' a firm base.

When you bounce, it is with tense taut legs to transfer the energy from an elastic bed into elevation of the body. Bouncing in the context of the following sequences is always a simultaneous double foot rebound from a sprung surface bed.

To ensure safety, the first skill children should be taught when exercising on any type of elastic bed is how to stop a rebound bounce. To land safely on a hard surface, a jumper must bend at the knees and hips to absorb the shock. Similarly a stop on a bouncette etc is created by bending/giving/relaxing at the knees and hips as soon as contact is made with the bed. This cushions the contact, keeps both feet on the bed and so negates bounce and rebound.

Bouncing on a sprung bed requires bilateral motor skills. Using both sides of the body and brain at the same time. This forces the body and brain to work together to maintain coordination and balance, therefore improving children's motor skills.

Equipment:

These bouncing activities are designed to help with sequencing – a core component of sentence construction.

A mini-tramp or bouncette [legs about 20–30 cms high] is used in order to keep the rebounds small – also about 20–30 cms. This keeps the time short between each element of the sequence.

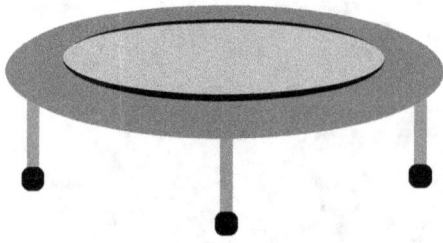

Sequences:

1. Six bounces, stop.
2. Five bounces, stop; ten bounces, stop.
3. Six bounces, stop; two bounces, stop.
4. Three bounces, kneel; three bounces, kneel.
5. Four bounces, sit; four bounces, sit.
6. Two bounces, kneel; five bounces, kneel.
7. Six bounces, sit; three bounces, sit.
8. Three bounces, kneel; three bounces, sit.
9. Four bounces, sit; four bounces, kneel.
10. Five bounces, kneel; two bounces, sit.
11. One bounce, sit: four bounces, kneel.
12. Three bounces, kneel, sit.
13. Four bounces, sit, kneel.
14. Five bounces, kneel, sit; five bounces, kneel, sit.
15. Six bounces, sit, kneel; six bounces, sit, kneel.
16. Two bounces, kneel, sit; seven bounces, kneel, sit.
17. Four bounces, kneel, sit; six bounces, sit, kneel.
18. Three bounces, sit, kneel; one jump, sit, kneel.
19. Six bounces, stop; seven bounces, stop; eight bounces, stop.

20. Three bounces, kneel; three bounces, kneel; three bounces, kneel.

21. Four bounces, sit. Three times.

22. Two bounces, kneel; five bounces, kneel; two bounces, kneel.

23. Four bounces, sit; two bounces, sit; six bounces, sit.

24. Two bounces, kneel; three bounces, sit; four bounces, kneel.

25. One bounce, sit; four bounces, kneel. Three times.

26. Three bounces, kneel, sit; four bounces, kneel, sit; five bounces, kneel, sit.

27. Eight bounces, kneel, sit; seven bounces, kneel, sit; six bounces, kneel, sit.

28. One bounce, kneel, sit; four bounces, sit, kneel.

29. Two bounces, sit, kneel. Three bounces, kneel, sit.

30. Four bounces, kneel, sit: One bounce, sit, kneel. Two times.

Make up your own sequences or ask the children to suggest a sequence.

Fine motor activities

Fine motor skills refer to precision, dexterity and coordination of the hands. These are the skills that allow us to use our hands to manipulate materials like pencils, containers, clothing fasteners and little objects.

There is so much more to it, though. Areas of development like bilateral coordination, pinch and grip strength, separation of the sides of the hand, arch development, finger isolation and thumb web space all play a role in refined use of the fingers and hands.

Fine motor skills gradually build for children as they do activities to help strengthen their muscles and coordination.

Activities:

Moulding clay or plasticine into a ball, a snake or various shapes.

Punching with a paper punch – random or set design.

Screwing and unscrewing nuts and bolts.

Picking up small objects one at a time e.g. buttons, beads, paper clips, pebbles.

Using clothes pegs:
- make a chain of pegs
- hanging clothes on a line.

Hand wring clothes.

Using granulated material e.g. sand, rice, beans, stones.

Passing small objects from person to person.

Stacking objects into piles.

Using locks and keys.

Dressing and undressing dolls or self.

Using paper clips to make a chain.

Threading or stringing beads.

Counting sticks or toothpicks – pick up one at a time.

Playing marbles.

Dropping objects into a bottle or tin.

Playing with building blocks and building objects.

Playing with Lego or Meccano sets.

Doing jigsaw puzzles.

Turning pages of a book.

Playing jacks (knuckles).

Making paper planes.

Gluing matchsticks to a board, tray or mat.

Knitting, use big needles and thick wool.

Knitting Nancy, cotton reel and nails.

Sewing – a line, a pattern or picture.

Screwing tops onto bottles.

Count a number of small objects picking up as many as possible with one hand e.g. beads, macaroni, small toys, buttons.

Finger painting.

Opening and closing safety pins.

Passing the bean bag from hand to hand or from person to person as quickly as possible.

Hitting balloons and keeping them in the air.

Throwing bean bags or large balls at targets.

'Bubble pipes' – blowing bubbles then bursting them with fingers.

Putting on and taking off gloves and socks.

Bowling at skittles.

Hitting a suspended ball – with the hand, a bat, a stick.

Playing musical instruments – piano, guitar, recorder.

Counting small objects on abacus or counting frame.

Dressing board – zips, press studs, hooks, buttons, laces.

Playing with nerf balls and nerf toys.

Ping pong balls – rolling, hitting from one end of the table to the other.

Tying and untying knots, bows, laces.

Post boxes – small box with slit in the top to post letters, cards, coins.

Picking up matches, pins and placing them in box, pin cushion.

Finger puppets, sock puppets, matchbox puppets.

Placing stickers.

Using a piano keyboard.

Playdoh, slime, plasticine, modelling clay, silly putty.

Patterns on cards – to be reproduced on peg boards.

Punching bag.

Using tweezers or tongs to pick up small objects e.g. peas, beads, buttons, smarties.

Spooning sand into wide mouth bottles.

Weaving and lacing activities, plaiting.

Basic woodwork, using simple tools.

Dealing out cards. Build a house of cards. Shuffling cards.

Dialling telephone numbers on toy phone.

Geoboards – nails on a board to make geometric shapes with rubber bands.

Pouring liquid from one container to another.

Matching pegs to strips of tape around top of ice-cream container.

Pushing toy cars along taped roads.

Hand tennis, basketball.

Making and flying kites.

Building a matchstick or icy-pole tower.

Counting or stacking coins with left and right hand.

Identify objects by touch – 'feel box'.

Making or copying patterns in a tray of sand.

Stringing cotton reels.

Printing – pieces of vegetables, hair rollers, pencils, leaves.

Collage – paper pieces, egg shells, buttons, bark, ceramics.

Making pipe cleaner animals.

Making paper balls – glue strips of paper into ball shape.

Magnets – pick up pins, nails, paper clips.

Making paper chains.

Making yarn balls or pom poms.

Imitating arm or finger actions – pretending to play a musical instrument.

Cooking:
- mixing ingredients with a spoon
- making pastry with hands
- using an eggbeater
- peeling oranges with fingers
- peeling apples with a peeler
- icing and decorating small cakes with hundreds and thousands
- washing and peeling vegetables.

Household jobs:
- washing and wiping dishes or packing and unpacking the dishwasher
- setting table
- dusting/vacuuming
- sorting and cleaning silverware.

Picking up various small objects from the floor with one hand at a time.

Transfer pegs with fingers from a row on pegboard to a container.

Catching quoits, bean bags small objects, soft balls.

Knots – children make different types of knots using string and rope of varying thickness.

Wrist exercises

Simple wrist exercises for children can help stretch and strengthen the wrist muscles and help the child use a good wrist-extended position when writing. In turn, this may help improve the child's fine motor skills and have a positive effect on handwriting.

Activities:

With forearm stabilised on a bench or a table, child moves hand up and down freely over the edge of the table – like a paint brush moving with vertical strokes.

Move hand freely from side to side.

Rotate the hand in a circular motion to the left and then to the right.

Move your wrist as if to screw and unscrew lids.

Strengthen wrist by playing restaurant and child is to carry a tray on an outstretched hand.

Practice crab walking.

Using a vertical surface can help children develop a good extended wrist position. Try painting, colouring a picture, rubbing a crayon flat over a picture, using stamps.

Hand and finger exercises

Muscle strength of the hands and fingers increases as children grow and participate in everyday activities. Hand and finger strength is important as it is required for many everyday activities and it also helps to develop the endurance to complete activities such as writing a full page.

Grip strength refers to whole hand strength. Pinch strength involves the thumb and index finger (and the middle finger if required).

These activities will help improve tone in the hands, increase stability in the thumb and fingers, develop and define arches of the hands, improve precision with in-hand manipulation and improve endurance in hand strength.

Activities:

Interlace fingers of both hands. Press palms hard together.

Make a fist and open it (both hands) out in front, above head, to the side.

Spread fingers apart fully then move them back together again.

Bring tip of thumb and each finger together successively – right hand, left hand, both hands, with eyes closed.

Extend fingers and thumb to maximum, hold for three seconds then relax.

Squeeze a small rubber ball rhythmically e.g. a nerf or stress ball.

Crumple rubbish paper into a ball. Begin on a flat surface and use only one hand; then crumple paper without the use of the flat surface.

Close fist and release one finger at a time; right hand, left hand, both hands.

Grasp tennis ball, then lift one finger at a time; right hand, left hand, both hands.

Bend shapes and angles from cardboard.

Extend hand and lower one finger at a time to form fist; right hand, left hand, both hands.

Open and close hand as fast as possible; right hand, left hand, both hands.

Place hand, palm down on the table with fingers together – move little finger as far away from the other fingers as you can – try to bring the ring finger to the little finger – then the other fingers one at a time.

Place fingers together – move thumb away and back again, then thumb plus index finger, then thumb, index plus great finger and finally all plus ring finger. Repeat with other hand.

Place hand, palm down on the table; make a fist, then lie it hard and flat.

Clayball rolling – two hands, one hand, four fingers, one finger, the thumb.

Tap rhythmic patterns with fingers.

Finger matching with hands placed heels together, touch together tips of each corresponding finger in order.

Finger clasping – with hand facing each other; children experiment different ways to clasp them together.

Place fingertips together and clap palms.

Place palm on table and tap each finger individually on the table.

String puzzles – string placed around the fingers; complete puzzles between fingers.

Cross middle fingers over pointer fingers; reverse, with pointer fingers over middle fingers.

Grasp hands with pointer finger of right hand between thumb and pointer finger of left hand. Interlace fingers.

Change, so that the pointer finger of left hand is between thumb and pointer finger of right hand. Interlace other fingers.

Finger plays and action games

Finger play and action games have existed for many years and have been passed down from generation to generation. These songs capture children's attention by pairing movement with the singing of simple songs like nursery rhymes. Engaging children in a finger play song is a simple way that you can help them develop and work on their fine motor skills while developing language skills.

Here is the church

Here is the church,
(interlock fingers on both hands with fingers in towards palms)

Here is the steeple,
(raise index fingers and touch at tips)

Open the doors,
(invert hands, fingers still interlocked, with backs of hands together)

And see all the people.
(wiggle all the interlocked fingers)

Ten little fingers

I have ten fingers,
(hold up both hands, fingers spread wide)

They all belong to me,
(point to self)

I can make them do things,
(hold up hands, wiggling fingers)

Would you like to see?

I can shut them up tight,
(make fists)

I can open them wide,
(open hands wide)

I can put them together,
(place palms of hands together)

I can make them hide.
(place hands behind your back)

I can make them jump high,
(raise hands over head)

I can make them jump low,
(touch hands to the floor)

I can fold them up quietly,
(fold hands in lap or in front)

And hold them just so!

Itsy bitsy spider

Itsy bitsy spider climbed up the water spout.
(lock thumbs together and let eight fingers crawl up.)
(older children can make circles out of thumbs and forefingers, put tips together and twist upward.)

Down came the rain,
(wiggle fingers in downward motion.)

And washed poor itsy out.
(push hands and arms forward in outward spreading motion.)

Out came the sun and dried up all the rain.
(make big circles with arms)

And itsy bitsy spider climbed up the spout again.
(fingers crawl up again.)

Mother's knives and forks

These are mother's knives and forks.
(fingers interlaced, tips up)

This is mother's table.
(flatten hands and arms)

This is mother's looking glass.
(palms toward face)

And this is baby's cradle.
(palms up, rock arms)

Where is Thumbkin?

Where is Thumbkin? Where is Thumkin?
(hide hands behind back)

Here I am! Here I am!
(show L thumb, then R thumb)

How are you today, sir?
(wiggle L thumb)

Very well, I thank you.
(wiggle R thumb)

Run away, run away.
(hide LH behind back, then RH)

2. Where is Pointer? ...
3. Tall man? ...
4. Ring man? ...
5. Little man (or pinkie)? ...

Open, shut them

Open, shut them,
(open hands then close them together)

Open, shut them,
give a little clap, clap, clap.
(clap hands each time you say 'clap')

Open shut them,
(open hands then close them together)

Open shut them,
lay them on your lap, lap, lap.
(tap your lap each time you say 'lap')

Creep them crawl them.
('crawl' fingers up the sides of your body)

Creep them crawl them,
right up to your chinnie, chin, chin.
(bring fingers to chin)

Open wide your little mouth,
but do not let them in.
(hide fingers behind back)

Finger dexterity activities

These finger exercises for kids are designed to increase the dexterity and skill of the tripod fingers, with the hope of ultimately improving children's pencil control and handwriting.

These fine motor activities are designed to be easily incorporated into a specialist session or the classroom program.

Activities:

20–30 matches in a matchbox – place the matches in the match box as quickly as possible.

Small clothes pegs – place the pegs around the top of shoebox, using index finger and thumb to open and close them.

Matches – make forms or shapes from sticks.

10 coins and 10 empty matchboxes – open each matchbox, place one coin and close. Start with coins in a box; take out coin, close box, place coin on top of box. Then replace coins.

Bolts, nut – screw ten nuts onto bolts as quickly as possible.

Coins, money box – place coins on various shapes and patterns, then post them into money box. Place coins in various positions in relation to money box; left, right, near, far.

Beads – threading beads as quickly as possible. Use large beads to begin with, then progress to smaller ones.

Lego pieces – fit pieces together as quickly as possible.

Make familiar shapes or objects as quickly as possible.

Scissors – cut as many circles out of paper as possible.

Using a square, cut around it to make as long a piece of paper as possible.

Tracing a maze without taking the pencil off the paper and staying within the lines.

Dropping marble into a bottle, using bottles with progressively smaller necks.

Stretching rubber bands over nails in various shapes.

Completing jigsaw puzzles.

Cutting activities

Cutting skills are quite complex and it takes time and practice for children to develop and master this skill. Scissor skills can help build hand and finger strength, develop skills necessary for fingers to work together which is also required to promote a functional pencil grasp which can increase pencil control and overall handwriting.

Activities:

Opening and closing scissors in a single movement.

Cutting along a line – short and thick.

Cutting along a continuous straight line or guidelines.

Cutting around curved lines.

Cutting to stop at line.

Cutting out shapes, geometric forms.

Cutting different materials.

Cutting fringes.

Tearing and cutting strips from old pieces of newspapers.

Cutting and pasting activities.

Cutting out magazine people.

Making scrap books – string, cutting, pasting.

Cutting out a long strip from a small square.

Cutting with left or right hand. Which is more difficult?

Cutting spirals.

Pre-writing activities

Pre-writing activities are a great place to start a child's handwriting journey. They can help build confidence creating lines and shapes and be valuable for helping to develop pencil control and steadiness of hand. Pre-writing activities are also useful for developing fine motor skills in children.

Activities:

Tracing around hands and feet.

Tracing around geometric shapes with one finger, crayon, pencil.

Dot to dot – placed either at random or in a sequence, pictures, shapes, letters, patterns etc.

Scribbling with large crayons on large pieces of paper.

Colouring within guidelines.

Negotiating a maze with a pencil.

Completing shapes or familiar objects.

Circle drawing – how many circles can you draw inside a 15 cm diameter circle?

Making rainbows by tracing over letters, shapes in five different colours.

Tracing around stencils, words, numbers and patterns.

Tracing maps or pictures and colouring.

Using mathematical instruments e.g. compass, set-square.

Tracing over letters.

Writing patterns with large crayons, chalk or textas.

Drawing activities

Drawing helps children develop fine motor skills by improving their hand-eye coordination. The more children practice to draw lines and figures, the faster they can improve their colouring and handwriting skills. There are many stages to drawing and some children need more activities to develop their drawing skills.

Activities:

Join dots with straight lines – increase distance between dots.

Large sweeping movements.

Draw a straight line from left to right, right to left.

Draw a circle.

Copy shapes or forms drawn by teacher.

Copy different line patterns.

Connect forms or different shapes with straight lines: variation of dot to dot.

Trace lines in different colours.

One child draws a wandering line on the board and the second child traces over the same pathway.

Make a clock; child connects a central dot with all the numbers on the clock face.

Join dots to form an object.

Copy patterns or designs.

Trace around templates.

Rule lines using a small ruler, and a blackboard ruler and colour them in.

Playing commercial games

Playing games is a great way to teach children how to co-operate and engage with others. It's an opportunity to hone their social skills as they learn the importance of sharing, fairness and teamwork.

In learning a new skill and completing an activity/winning a game, a child will feel extremely proud, and will experience a real boost in their confidence and self-esteem.

Children learn more than just the language of the lesson when playing a game. They may learn instructional language, rules and sometimes develop negotiation skills. Children can form a greater variety of emotional connections with language through playing games

Games:

Pick-up sticks

Marble run

Draughts

Barrel of Monkeys

Yo-yo

Spirograph

Origami

Chinese checkers

Chess

Three-dimensional nought and crosses

Pocket solitaire

Jacks or knuckles

Stamp albums

Magnet sets

Nerf balls

Quoits

Hooky

Pegboards

Interlocking toys

Construction sets and construction blocks – buckets of bricks, Lego, Meccano, magna tiles

Twister

Interlocking circles

Connect Four

Cheap activity books from supermarkets and newsagents

Concentration

Ludo

Rubik's Cube

Zingo!

Pop Up Pirate!

Jenga/tumbling tower

Snakes and ladders

Dominoes

Picture dominoes

Jigsaw puzzles

Card Games – Old maid, Snap, Donkey etc.

www.ingramcontent.com/pod-product-compliance
Lightning Source LLC
Chambersburg PA
CBHW070054120526
44588CB00033B/1425